VIENNA

VIENNA

PORTRAIT OF A METROPOLY

PHOTOGRAPHS BY
MANFRED HORVATH

INTRODUCTION BY
HELMUT ZILK

VERLAG CHRISTIAN BRANDSTÄTTER · VIENNA – MUNICH

THE PULL OF THE INELUCTIBLE

I might as well admit it straightaway: these lines are the admission of a life long love affair. The object of this love is the city of my birth; a long-suffering beauty, whose vitality pulses and flows like the waters of the great river that traverses it. What is Vienna? What makes Vienna special? And how can this "specialness" be made more tangible? "Vienna is like a pocket knife", were the words of Helmut Qualtinger

whose attitude to the city mixed love and pain in equal measure: often enough, just real pain. But it gets even worse: "Vienna is like a pocket knife under a heaven full of hangovers". A city that throbs, which is more often than not constricted by that wonderfully beautiful but rather narrow corset known as Austria, so that the firmament is indeed full of headache. And what if these are just imagined pains? What would that change for us, the Viennese?

It takes subtle psychological analysis to unravel the conflicting forces at work in this city. It is no coincidence that the city is situated on the middle stretch of the Danube, a river that flows through much of the continent. For hundreds of years travellers from many parts of Europe reached the Vienna Basin by following the river or one of the ancient trade routes that crossed it. Only to settle there in the mild Pannonian cli-

Title page: the view from the roof of the Parliament building with the Leopoldine Wing of the Hofburg in the background. pp. 4 & 5: one of the rooftop quadrigae of the Parliament building with its Winged Victory in the foreground and the City Hall (left) and Votive Church in the background. pp. 6/7: the Lipizzaner horses with their manes braided for a gala performance. pp. 8/9; Schubert's birthplace in Nussdorferstrasse; his reading spectacles are preserved in a glass showcase. pp. 10/11: "Swan Lake" at the Opera, the cast take the final bow. pp. 12/13: View from the vaults into the nave of St. Stephen's Cathedral. pp. 14/15: the Imperial Treasury in the Hofburg; the showcase contains the crown of Rudolf II. (the Austrian Imperial Crown) and the Imperial Orb and Sceptre, Friedrich Amerling's portrait of Emperor Franz I hangs on the wall. pp. 16/17: the Giant Ferris Wheel illuminated at night. pp. 18/19: Vienna's modern skyline across the Danube is dominated by the Andromeda Tower and the Vienna International Centre ("UNO City").

Opposite: guests at the Opera Ball refreshing themselves between dances. Above: Vienna's silhouette as a backdrop to the Opera Ball.

mate. Thus, from the beginning many invisible arteries emanated from and converged on Vienna.

It is no coincidence that Europe's two cerebral hemispheres met in Vienna and that occasionally mental waves are reflected back – although this was rarely the view taken in Vienna. It is no coincidence that Vienna is probably the world capital of self-castigation. It should be no surprise that self-castigation is virtually a pan-European pastime or at least a German, Austrian, Bohemian and Hungarian one. And because Vienna represents an admixture of the aforesaid ingredients, in this part of the world one always holds a large grinder ready into which, above all, those elements that do not really deserve to be grinded down are shoved with great virtuosity and a considerable amount of accompanying lamentation.

Lamentation in the face of lament? Nothing of the sort. The Viennese knows himself well enough even on the threshold of self-consciousness. The navel of Austria, of Europe, even the whole world. Austria erit in orbe ultima. It is no coincidence that the world's best orchestra is located here I hope that the other great orchestras will forgive my presumption. It is no coincidence that the pitch of musical instruments in Vienna differs from that of the rest of the world by fractions of a semitone. Vienna allows itself the luxury of tuning its oboes to 444 hertz instead of 440. Is that the secret of our proverbial musicality? Musicality seems to be a special pair of chromosomes in the genetic material of the Viennese. Nevertheless, most of the Viennese including, I would say, an above-average number of bright people have restricted themselves to that most Viennese of concert pitches namely, grumbling. It is no coincidence that Vienna is renowned as the city of psychoanalysis or at least the capital city of repression. But it is also the world capital of medicine: each of the three Viennese schools of medicine moulded medical science for generations, indeed centuries.

But who would resent our having complicated souls with impenetrable mechanisms? The Viennese soul is a surrogate for the history of the city. Its spiritual manifestations are the distillate of a sophisticated mix of ingredients. – and no one has ever succeeded in draining this distillate in one gulp. Thus, Vienna best reveals itself in small sips – in the certain knowledge that this rare elixir will suffice for future generation of Vienna cognoscenti.

It is no coincidence that this city was the actual (or at least spiritual refuge) of those living behind the Iron Curtain who found their own circumstances distressingly constricted. This, of course, included more than just a handful of artists, authors and actors. But Vienna willingly opened its big heart even to the arts' voluntary expatriates: those who think mentioning Beethoven (who was born in Bonn, but landed in Vienna) and the Hanse Brahms (who chose Vienna as his home) to be too obvious should be reminded of Claus Peymann and his well-oiled marketing machine which ran for many years and which he powered from the most prestigious German language theatre, the Burgtheater. It is not merely since the advent of Peymann and again no coincidence that theatre reviews always seem to wind up in the political columns in this country. And aren't politics, more often than not (and more often than is good for them), a little like a theatre rehearsal, representing merely a tentative option on reality?

It is no coincidence that this city, this country, refused

entry to the members of the ruling family of the ancien régime for three decades: a fear of imaginary dangers, a kind of collective hypochondria, always had the upper hand over well-founded fears in Vienna. In fact, the Viennese like to close their eyes to real dangers, which is why so many, far too many, swore eternal allegiance to the "Führer" (who returned to the city after leaving Vienna full of venom at his own rejection) and his crusade of mass destruction throughout Europe. But at the same time, it is no coincidence that this city is one of the three cities to house the headquarters of the United Nations, an organisation which (to paraphrase Churchill's bon mot about democracy) leaves much to be desired but unfortunately has no real alternative. We are said to have a special talent for political mediation since the Kreisky era to counterbalance this. It is no coincidence that Vienna ranks third among the list of most attractive conference venues in the world. What does Vienna mean to me, what is my Vienna? I have to admit one thing: my love has only grown fonder as a result of its hidden thorns and barbs. In all the years I have been living and working here, I opened my heart more and more and in the final analysis have fallen irrevocably for this city. And it dawned on me that whoever tries hard enough to win the affection of this city will be rewarded in the end.

Even today, seven decades after I set foot on a Vienna pavement hand-in-hand with my father (in the Eighth District, the Josefstadt, the area of the city I grew up in) every time I arrive back from abroad, I am filled with the same feeling of diffident pride. Unquestionably, every return to one's home is also a form of self-communion. But only very few cities exude the same heady atmosphere constituted from all of its stories, its stories and destinies, which turn any arrival into an eternally recurring and thrilling rendezvous. Few cities have been able to curb the unfettered growth, the excess, the neurosis of urban life so successfully and consistently as Vienna. Few cities rest on such solid foundations. Few receive the new with such equanimity, but without turning their backs on the opportunities of the future this, however, is usually received with the comment "we've been through this before". Few cities are, as far as their own re-creation, their reproduction in the course of the centuries is concerned, so autonomous, so self-confident in the defence of their roots, their essence, their inner structure. Any newcomer to Vienna will immediately grasp that this is such a city.

Technology allows us to experience cities and landscapes in a way that was barred to earlier generations. The approach to Vienna airport can be a breath-taking and exciting affair when the pilot is forced to comply with weather conditions by flying over the city: Otto Wagner's Steinhof Church appears unexpectedly on the left, then Schönbrunn Palace on the right and shortly afterwards the whole city is spread below. One thing immediately becomes apparent: Vienna's air is much clearer than that of many cities of comparable size. This is not merely because of such recent developments as the ambitious plan of a long-distance heating system, or the filter technology installed in modern power plants; nor is it merely the result of the environmentally friendly use of tram lines (known as the "Tramway" or "Electrical", as it is known by the older generation, and more and more frequently by the onomatopoetic appellation "Bim"), nor the fleet of public busses powered by liquid gas (clearly recognizable from the grey hump on their roof, which stores the fuel). No, Vienna profits from its climatic situation between different landscape zones, which is so conducive to winds. West of the city are the foothills of the Alps; the Vienna Woods and the Danube Valley are situated to its north, creating a natural wind machine whose bellows is directed towards the dry Pannonic area of the Vienna Basin to the south and the great Central European Plain situated to the east.

Wind is one of the constant factors in the city, particularly in the spring and autumn. Although this might cause occasional vexation to anyone sporting a hat, it has a very beneficial effect on the city's air circulation; Vienna has little experience with that scourge of most modern cities, smog. Thus the view from such a lofty perspective is an ideal introduction for incoming visitors hoping to spend a few days by the Danube.

Vienna undoubtedly also has ideal qualities for a rendezvous at ground level. These are set off to best advantage when one approaches the city from the west. The highway has just been meandering through the clusters of Flysch hills of the Vienna Woods, but suddenly, almost without transition, one is plunged into the sea of houses that is Vienna. Apart from its southern approaches, which have begun to assume the character of a succession of hyper stores, car dealers and drive-ins of all descriptions familiar from suburban America, the metropolis on the Danube begins and ends rather abruptly at all its other perimeters. These are formed by the bright and cheery urban developments of the nineties to the north and east, interspersed by the economic and architectural austerity characteristic of a more frugal epoch. The northwest is marked by the unusual intrusion of new high-rise buildings along the banks of the Danube that tower over the vintner's houses in the wine-growing regions of Kahlenbergerdorf and Nussdorf.

Vienna is bedded in a topography that seems to have been arranged by a loving hand. The Vienna Woods and its fringes north of the Danube, the Bisamberg, form a shallow scallop-like basin that flattens out towards the south-east and in which the city is ensconced. If one gazes from the slopes of the Vienna Woods down towards the city, the ground falls by stages with one or the other foothill of the mountainous terrain at the viewer's back partially covered with suburban villas, sometimes with vineyards basking in the sunlight intruding into the foreground. This, too, is an example of the sensitive utilisation of the landscape: about 30% of the area of Vienna is cultivated for the purposes of agriculture and forestry. This is an indication of the absurdity of the short-lived "thousand year" expansion of Greater Vienna in recent history to combine surrounding towns, villages and fields to form a total of 26 districts. As it is, some of Vienna's traditional number of 23 districts have an extraordinarily bucolic air and are, as it were, agriculturally autonomous indeed, the tasty vegetables grown in Vienna are also eaten in Graz and Linz. Not to mention Viennese wines …

The gentle montane topography of the Vienna Woods penetrates inexorably beyond the city limits: even if Vienna's hills and dales do not reveal the dramatic sequence of the Seven Hills of Rome, there is hardly a street in the south of Vienna without an incline or decline. Superficially, the wide expanse of roofs disguises this up and down motion: but if one goes on foot through the city valleys, like those of the rivers

Wien and Als, it become very apparent. Even in the south, in the transition area to the level Viennese Basin, the Laaerberg and Wienerberg represent a gentle barrier to the surrounding hinterland. A succession of ice ages have left terraces in the landscape in those areas where the spurs of the Vienna Wood can no longer reach to disrupt the flatness of the terrain. Thus, even the approach to the city from the south awards us with a raised view of the bright lights of the city at night: many who approach the city via the so-called Rauchenwarter Platte will be surprised not to perceive Vienna as a reflection of its own flood of lights but, for a few minutes at least, as a gleaming sea spread out in the distance. The same applies to those who approach the city from the north, not by following the streets along the valley floors but by crossing the tilting plateau between Korneuburg and Stockerau by side roads. By the way, this almost represents the historical perspective of the former Imperial Residence, because the foreground of the majestic monastery in Klosterneuburg is a reminder that this area was the seat of the Babenberg dukes for long decades and that its political significance greatly outweighed that of the medieval city of Vienna to its rear.

Guests to our city are attracted by the high points of architectural history. But it would seem sensible to choose a traditional form of travel namely, on foot, or at least at ground level. It is only then that the secret magic that Vienna weaves on both its residents and guests can enfold, although its presence seems much more arbitrary than in many other cities. The magic spell of sudden vistas, of axes (to which the builders of the Baroque era and later devoted whole dissertations, and who demonstrated this by conceiving entire ideal cities). These axes seem to have just happened in Vienna and there are dozens that can eternally charm the Viennese and cognoscenti of Vienna. The visual axes in and through Vienna, that direct the eyes to those places where this city has set its eternal anchor. Schönbrunn, Kahlenberg, jewels such as the water tower in Favoriten, or the steeples of the Baroque Viennese churches and again and again the "Steffl", as the Viennese affectionately call St. Stephen's Cathedral.

Hardly any other cathedral manifests its significance for a country, a nation, in such a clear and organic manner as this mediaeval spatial and structural wonder. It looms alone and at a lofty height over the warren of narrow streets that make up the old city of Vienna. This part of town has hardly any high-rise buildings. Despite the fact that they are increasingly springing up along an arm of the Danube that has been dammed up to form a reservoir for power supply, the centre of the city will remain free of architectural excesses. The roof of the cathedral caught fire in 1945, its interior was badly damaged by collapsing masonry and the largest bell in the country, the "Pummerin", fell to the floor: the terrible din caused by the crashing bell weighing 20 tonnes marked the final dissonance in six years of senseless and vicious murder. The reconstruction of the cathedral was organised and carried out by people who often lacked even basic needs, but whose donations revealed an enormous and concerted national effort. Its reconstruction says more about the conditio austriae than any scientific study can. When the Viennese and the Austrian repossessed their "Steffl" every federal province made its own contribution to the repairs and the words of the great Viennese psychiatrist Alfred Adler were vindicated once more:

"There is no general truth. But what comes closest to it is community".

I myself was made deeply and painfully aware of the consequences of rejecting the idea of community when, at the age of eleven and at my father's side, I saw the synagogue in the Neudeggergasse in the Josefstadt, just a stone's throw from my parents' apartment, go up in flames. The November pogrom of 1938 was followed by the exodus of 120,000 Viennese Jews and the murder of another 60,000.

The Jewish Museum in Vienna, the oldest and most historic of its kind in Europe, was another victim of the Nazi hordes. It was left to our generation to make a new start with the victims, with the remaining small Jewish congregation. One of the happiest moments in my political career was when I was able to welcome Teddy Kollek, Jerusalem's long-standing mayor who was born in Vienna, to Vienna's Municipal Council. His friendly words to the representatives gathered there were only possible because the rules governing parliamentary procedure were bent a little. Kollek later returned and we opened the new Jewish Museum in Vienna together in 1993: an institution that has done extraordinarily well since then and which in turn shows just how necessary the revival of this museum would prove to be. A further focal point of the Viennese and, indeed, Austrian soul is situated nearby at the end of the Kärntnerstrasse. When the Vienna State Opera was re-opened in 1955, after 10 years' Allied occupation and reconstruction, millions sat in front of their wirelesses and were deeply moved by the broadcast of "Fidelio". Not that this country comprises of millions of music enthusiasts; no, this was an eloquent testimony to the national consensus that better times lay ahead.

Apropos appreciation of art: the fine arts have often been neglected in the city of Klimt, Kokoschka and Wotruba, but are now enjoying a long-deserved boom. However, it is part of the makeup of the Viennese and their natural and nonchalant approach to masterpieces that they hardly took any notice of the extraordinary number of Bruegel paintings – to name just one master that can be found in Vienna – until they were re-hung for a special exhibition and decked out with a few token loans from abroad. Before and afterwards, it is quite possible for a visitor to Vienna with a modest enthusiasm for art to inform an educated but somewhat ignorant Viennese of the treasures the city's collections have to offer. The Viennese then carefully conceals his surprise in order to say with appropriate pride: "Well, you know that's just Vienna: enough culture to feed the pigs with, as Torberg's Aunt Jolesch might put it!" The plain fact of the matter is the normal Viennese hardly ever voluntarily sets foot inside the Kunsthistorisches Museum after absolving the obligatory school outing there as a child. But there is justifiable hope that this partial obtuseness might be cured with the aid of the new Museum Quarter.

All of this should not divert our attention from the fact that the Viennese only really feel at home when their creature comforts are adequately catered for. Ergo, the guest to Vienna should transfer his studies at the earliest possible opportunity to those places where the real soul of the city is to be found: in its "Beisls", the traditional Viennese restaurants. Ever since the original Viennese allowed others to settle in their city, and ever since a handful of newcomers (behind their standard-bearer Wolfram Siebeck) acquired the necessary knowledge of the local culinary topology, this enterprise is no longer as time and labour consuming for the uninitiated as it once was. Like a perfect walking tour, which does not just end in blisters but hopefully in deeper perception, beisl tours in these parts hang from the silken thread of the expertise of an experienced Sherpa.

So what makes Vienna so special? How can it be articulated? Is it reflected in a soup bowl, in what fits between a knife and fork? In an enjoyable evening at the State Opera? In a Sunday morning in summer spent in the still sleepy old city, before the noonday sun has heated pavements and pedestrians? In an evening in a heurige, a local vineyard, that ends in tipsiness and temptation? In figures, fates, people, historical dates, stories? Maybe in pictures, whose pure and clear key leaves room for any number of the melodic lines that Vienna continually inhales and exhales?

Vienna, at the close of this eventful century, has more than proven its ability to survive and thrive. This was accompanied by a good deal of savoir vivre in the prosperous decades of the recent past, and a great deal of joie de vivre, an extraordinary amount of open-mindedness, any amount of self-confidence, and, especially, plenty of curiosity. Thus, in combination with the perpetuum mobile of its incomparable history, this Vienna would seem invulnerable in every sense. Protected by best wishes for its past greatness hovering in the world's ether and hardly affected by the imprecations of a few disappointed souls. Put into the right light by the criticism of its true acolytes, the magnanimous, the successful failures, the secret world champions, the rogues and honest souls. Protected from the pettiness of the Beckmessers of this world, supported by the caryatids of reputation, the real and eternal authorities. Upholstered with the love of all of those, whose relationship to the city has reached a stage where they have the illusion or, indeed, the unshakeable conviction of being able to avail of the privilege of their love being requited. In the safekeeping of the many whose contribution to the city has not been carved in stone, not printed on paper, nor extolled by anyone.

I may in all humility request dispensation at this juncture. To say what is different about Vienna, would first require saying what is different about my Vienna. And I was afforded the privilege of playing a prominent role in the building of my Vienna for many years. A more partisan stance could hardly be imagined.

Thus, I will merely say one thing, but this with absolute conviction: this city deserves to be loved.

HELMUT ZILK

CITY WITHOUT SURETY!

Let me not speak of any random city but of the only one in which my fears and hopes from so many years were caught in a net. I can still see it sitting by the broad, even-tempered river like a big, slatterny fisherwoman, pulling in its silvery and putrefried catch. Silvery the fear, putrefied the hope.

By the black water of the Danube and the chestnut sky above the mould-green domes:

Let me sweep out something of your good spirit from the dust and surrender your evil spirit to the dust! Then may the wind come and sweep away a heart that was proud and offended here!

City of flotsam and jetsam!

For countries were washed up on you and goods from other countries: the cross-stitch embroidery of the Slovaks and the pitchy moustaches of the Montenegrins, the egg-basket of the Bulgars and a rebellious accent from Hungary. City of the Turkish moon! City of the barricades!

So much crumbled stone, so many hollow walls are there that you can hear a whispering that comes from long ago, from far away.

O all the nights that came about in Vienna, so many bitter nights! And all the days that it threw to you accompanied by the buzz from schools and mental hospitals, from old age homes and sickrooms, litte aired and rarely painted with white paint, all the days around which shy chestnut blossoms swarm! O all the windows that never opened, all the gates as though there were no way out through any gate, as though the sky didn't exist.

Terminal city! As though no railway line ran out of it! An atmosphere of aulic councillors and retirement in government offices. Never a harsh word in the anterooms, always a hurtful one. (Always delay, never dismiss.)

There is the question of whether one has to love what one does not want to love, but the city is beautiful and a ceremonious poet climbed onto the tower of St. Stephen's and paid homage to it.

It is all a question of giving way, of concurrence. But some drank the cup of hemlock unconditionally. Evil report has entered into agreement with the soft heart. But some had a heart with a wild jocular muscle and a speech that would have been accepted in Rome. They were hostile, hated and lonely. They thought precisely, kept themselves pure and left the scum to themselves.

Preceding pages: View from the Leopoldsberg towards the south-east with the Danube, Danube Island and "Transdanubia", (as the other bank of the river is known to the Viennese). Above: the skyline of Vienna with St. Stephen's Cathedral illuminated at night.

A few had words at their disposal which they send like fireflies into the approaching night and over the frontiers. And one had a forehead that glowed blue and tragic between the tides of speechlessness.

City of the pyre, in which the most magnificent music is thrown into the flames, in which that which came from the upright heretics, the impatient suicides, the thorough discoverers, and everything that originated from the most honest spirit, is spat upon and slandered.

City of silence! Mute inquisitress with the non-committal smile.

– but the sobbing from loose cobblestones when someone staggers over them, flayed by silence, murdered by smiling. Where to with the cry rising out of the tragedy?

City of actors! City of frivolous angels and a handful of demons ripe for the pawnshop.

Shy city in dialogue, shy germ in a conversation of tomorrow.

City of wits, of lickspittels, of boon companions. (For the point of a joke a truth is sacrificed and well said is half lied.) Plague city with the smell of death!

By the black water of the Danube and the dirty oil in the distance:

Let me think of the radiance of a day that I have also seen, green and white and sober, after fallen rain,
when the city was washed and purified,
when the streets ran out star-shaped
from its core, its strong heart, purified,
when the children on every floor
began to practise a new étude,
when the trams came back from the Central Cemetery with all the wreaths and bunches of asters from the previous year,
because there was resurrection,
from death,
from oblivion!

INGEBORG BACHMANN

View from the City Hall to the Burgtheater, with the spires of the Cathedral, St. Michael's, the Church of the Minorites and the Michaelerkuppel of the Hofburg.

33

VIENNA ECHOING

Vienna – echoing
below the hills:
the year-long
note of an oboe.

Vienna – echoing stone,
soft-sounding major-key stone
in tune with the river,
a chorale in green.

Vienna – stillness echoing
across the water,
like a breath
before dying.

Vienna – the scent of reeds,
helpless before the wind,
laid low below the hills,
between azure vaults
and the uncertain meadows.

Vienna long-echoing love
that begins to sound from within me.

GASTONE BIGGI

The Hofburg, the labyrinthine centre of power of the old
Dual Monarchy, now houses numerous scientific and artistic collections.
Opposite: the Imperial Apartments, with the statue of Empress Elisabeth
by Hermann Klotz in the background. Above: Maria Theresia's apartments.

STREETS OF VIENNA

I wear out good shoe leather,
Vienna's pavements trudging.
Columns, arches together
Watch me pass by,
ungrudging.

Fat caryatids, presented
On pillars by the way,
Seem very well contented
To see me back today.

A wasteland of disorder
Where once green gardens
grew,
I will not cross their border
To tread that desert through.

Tritons and naiads graven
In swelling robes of stone.
Many have found safe haven,
Though others now lie prone.

The Graben's old plague
pillar,
Unbombed, still towers high.
Not every airborne killer
Has passed Vienna by.

Today, silently, lightly,
The snow has grasped the
crown,
And innocence lies whitely
On countryside and town.

BERTHOLD VIERTEL,

Court etiquette. Above: the dining room with its lavishly decked table in the Imperial Apartments.
Opposite: a detail of the Imperial table featuring elaborately folded serviettes and bread rolls.

Above: Hofburg, Imperial Silver Collection; a glass showcase with porcelain tableware.
Opposite: Hofburg; Collection of Old Musical Instruments, a violin featuring a portrait of Emperor Franz Joseph.

VIENNA, VIENNA, VIENNA

I am so proud that I'm a real Viennese!
I am so proud I'm not from Helsinki or Rome!
I'm no Hungarian, no Bulgarian, no Chinese,
I'm no Brasilian, no Sicilian, Pekingese,
I call Vienna my unquestionable home.

And I am proud that I'm so proud of my home town,
and I am proud that I'm proud that that's the case,
because of all the towns Vienna is the crown,
and I'm from there and not some other stupid place.

Can you imagine just how proud I really am?
Can you imagine why I sparkle, shine and glow?
I'm not just proud, I'm also happy as a clam,
I'm from Vienna just in case
you didn't know.

Oh my Vienna, oh my Vienna,
Vienna, Vienna, Vienna, Vienna!
Oh my! Oh my! Oh my! Oh my!
Vienna! Vienna! Vienna! Vienna!

GEORG KREISLER

Preceding pages: The restoration of old ivory medallions is very delicate work.
Above: the Heldenplatz with a view of the new wing of the Hofburg containing the National Library,
Ephesos Museum and the Collection of Old Musical Instruments. Above right: the Inner Castle Yard with the Statue
of Emperor Franz I. Below right: a detail of the equestrian statue of Prince Eugene of Savoy in Heldenplatz.

A LETTER REACHES ME FROM VIENNA

A letter reaches me from Vienna, on behalf of the Austrian National Library, Vienna 1, Heldenplatz, Corps de logis (Ringtrakt) of the New Imperial Palace,

from Working Counsellor of State Dr. Walter G. Wieser, Director of the Picture Archive and Portrait Collection:

"Dear Sir or Madam, The portrait collection of the Austrian National Library is endeavouring to establish an advantage over pure graphic art collections by emphasising the documentary nature of its iconographic holdings and so is in a position to consider not only engravings beyond the natural limits of a copper engraving cabinet but also photographs. However, the possibility of preserving a link with the times in this manner encounters the difficulty of obtaining photographs of contemporary personalities for want of an appropriate market. The portrait collection believes that the

"Dance seems to have been born here: created by man and horse together" (Otto Stoessl): hardly anyone can resist the appeal of the Spanish Riding School. Above: practising a cruciform quadrille. Below: a courbette. Opposite: a capriole.

only feasible manner in which it can continue to maintain the universality of human achievement in all fields and all ages, as represented in its stock of over 750,000 portraits, is by addressing individual requests to those personalities whose international standing makes it desirable for their portraits to be preserved in the collection. The collection is therefore pleased to number your good self among those to whom this request has been made. Your portrait reproduced by any technology, with the exception of a half-tone print, preferably an unlaminated photograph (7-by-5 inch format, or larger or smaller) would be welcome for the abovementioned purpose. We should also be very particularly grateful for an autograph memorandum of your essential biographical data and, if possible, the name of the photographer and the year in which the portrait was taken, either on the back of the photograph if possible or on a separate sheet which could be passed on to our autograph collection. The portrait collection tenders its most sincere thanks in advance for your kind consideration of this request. The Director." Praise be to Real Counsellor of State Wieser! May his melodiously melancholic affectations of style be eulogised in long post-Dodereresque ages! Blessed be he who, even at the non-negligible risk of losing his connection to passing or passed time within its natural limits, is still doing his best to favour those accessible word-pictures and word-structures, beauteous as the fixed stars, which, alas, even in Vienna

have long since been swept away by the muddy waters of the Danube; and indeed shows himself estimably inclined, self-revealingly, to a keenly desirable and impeccably careful extent, towards the flower of universality of distressingly human futility as such in every region.

I at any rate have hastened to seize the advantage offered me and sent Wieser my photo, sorry photograph, my accessible c.v. and at the same time my captivated high-minded soul, to Vienna, to the Heldenplatz.

ECKHARD HENSCHEID

Above: the Great Hall of the National Library is one of the most beautiful library rooms in the world.
Above left: Emperor Franz Joseph's Reading Room. Below left: the "Fideicommissum" Library.

Above: the Michaelerkuppel rises over the new wing of the Hofburg. The designs for this part of the Hofburg
go back to the 18th century but could only be realised towards the end of the last century.
Right: the Maria Theresia Monument by Caspar von Zumbusch in the square
between the Kunsthistorisches and Naturhistorisches Museum.

48

DECLARATION TO VIENNA

Can the exile well set down
A love song, grave yet gay,
To forgotten childhood's town,
A city far away?
Because you never slake my thirst
I drink to you tonight –
That it was you that fed me first,
Vienna, that's all right.

You stole my father from me when
Twilight was glimmering.
Dying, they brought him home again,
He lies in Simmering.
Whether your pulse beats in my head,
Or whether that distant light
Has died that you conceal my dead,
Vienna, that's all right.

My boyhood years were spent in you,
Long nights' enticements came.
My manhood's fires have burned me through
While you did fan the flame.
Despite your girlhood's long decay
To poverty and blight -
That you took my innocence away,
Vienna, that's all right.
You watched me through my growing pains,

Then cast me out to roam.
Only a man with ice-filled veins
Clings to a burning home.
And when the days of thirty-eight
Set shame and rage alight –
That you forced me to an exile's fate,
Vienna, that's all right.

Because I now dwell far from you,
Your picture blurs, until
Sometimes it's all that I can do
To see your image still.
You my delight and you my pain, Anxiety
and fright –
That I should see you once again,
Vienna, that's all right.

ERICH FRIED

Mortality is one of the recurring elements in the Viennese view of life. Above the caskets in the Imperial Crypt in the Capuchin Church have to be continually restored to guard against pewter corrosion. Above left: the crypt of St. Michael's Church contains some mummified bodies of the 18th century. Below left: the hearts of the Habsburgs were interred in the "Herzgrüftel" ("Hearts' Sepulchre") in the Augustine Church, their bodies in the Crypt of the Capuchins and their viscera in the crypt of St. Stephen's Cathedral.

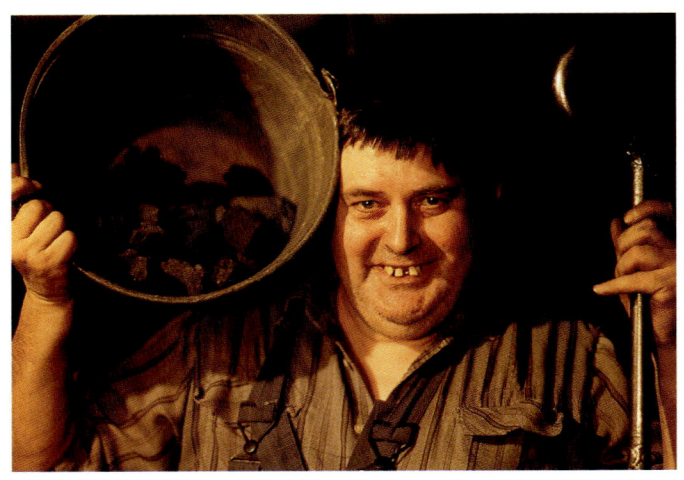

VIENNESE

Gently nasal, soft as an eavesdropper
Among all the German dialects,
Light, sweet yet dangerous, like sparkling
Sekts
Among wines, lacking that proper
Prussian rasp, that clarion call to duty,
But very melodious, sensitive to beauty,

That's my Viennese from Ottakring,
The accent I picked up in childhood there,
Songs that from hurdy-gurdies filled the air,
Songs that even now in dreams I sing,
My language, lilting and light-tripping,
Gracefully still into my new tongue slipping,

Colouring every English sound I make
In my new country, handing it down
The softness of the old, of my home town,
And melancholy's soft, inner voice must take
Its toll, inhabiting every alien word,
My origin hinted, never quite unheard.

ERNST WALDINGER

Above: the city's subterranean sewer system was made world famous by Carol Reed's film "The Third Man".
Above left: a stoker in the Floriani Tröpferlbad (a public bathhouse) in the Eighth District.
Below left: a coal dealer in the Leopoldstadt.

The painter Friedensreich Hundertwasser was able to implement his concept of organic construction in a number of building projects in the federal capital. Above: the façade of the incinerator at Spittelau. Below right: a detail of the Spittelau incinerator.

HUNDERTWASSER

Hundertwasser was the name of a painter
who lived in modern times.
You could say ultramodern really
He was so close to our time.
He was known for his circularities
in his pictures.
He had a modern-day viewpoint
Looking at images.
His painting entered into the history
of pictorial research.
In private life he enjoyed schnitzel
and had a very sweet tooth.
Women knew him too and
he enjoyed their respect.
Different pictures yielded a reflex.

EDMUND MACH

Modern architecture is becoming more commonplace in the streets of Vienna.

Above: an elementary school in Köhlergasse in the 18th District (Hans Hollein, architect).

Above right: the Kunsthalle in Karlsplatz (Adolf Krischanitz, architect). Below right (left): the pilot project for

a housing development in the 22nd District. (Krischanitz, Steidle and Partners, Herzog and de Meuron, architects).

Below extreme right: Ludwig Wittgenstein designed this house in the Third District for his sister, Margarete Stonborough.

MARBLE-CHRONICLE

The world L. builds for may be bad,
But his materials are fine.
Although its downfall would be sad,
The ruins remaining still will shine.
For marble keeps the glow it had.
History is a mine
of tales of luxury run mad,
where jackals dine;
they plundered here the bad
money we paid the fine.
Mid opals' shine
whence falls the light's glad
grace on smoke and battle line,

everything lay there, empty, sad,
before the journals' sign
and had those it does not send mad
envisage death's design
and drove him out, we had
husks upon husks in line
as like and like gladly align.
O see the hostelries, such fine
buildings for swine.
L. gave them what they had!

KARL KRAUS

VIENNA

vienna's like a lover
that steals away while you're
asleep
a cry that you strangle
a knife that is too blunt
to thrust into a heart
vienna is a bloodstream
that freezes in the veins
an extinguished light
a lonely bullet
above the abandoned

*Opposite: the new Haas House (Hans Hollein, architect)
in Stephansplatz has become one of the sights of Vienna.
Above left and below left: Wilhelm Holzbauer designed this
bank outlet in Lassallestrasse and the Andromeda Tower
beside the UNO City. Below right: the Karl Marx Hof in
the 19th District is perhaps the most famous example
of the council housing projects erected by the Socialist
government in Vienna in the inter-war years.
Above right: the IBM Building
(Wilhelm Holzbauer, architect).*

battlefield whizzing
you cannot trap vienna
like a rat or snap it off
from a row of rotten teeth
you know no necessity
to feel at home
you live as in a graveyard
of furniture and wallpaper
vienna is no more than a birdsong
that you sing in mockery
or sadly to a zither's tune
floating into your house
on the windless air
vienna is a revolt
sinking into the sand
when you talk of vienna
you no longer talk of yourself

WALTER BUCHEBNER

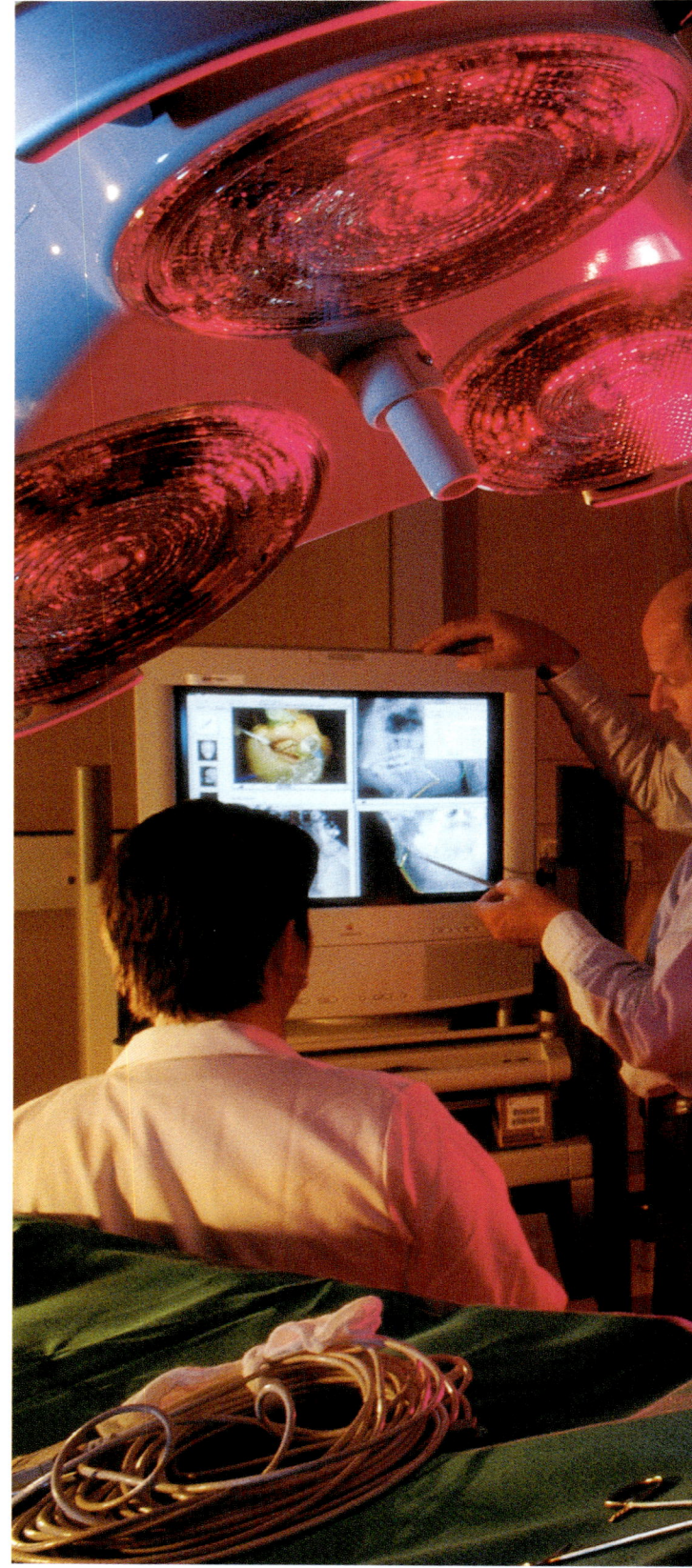

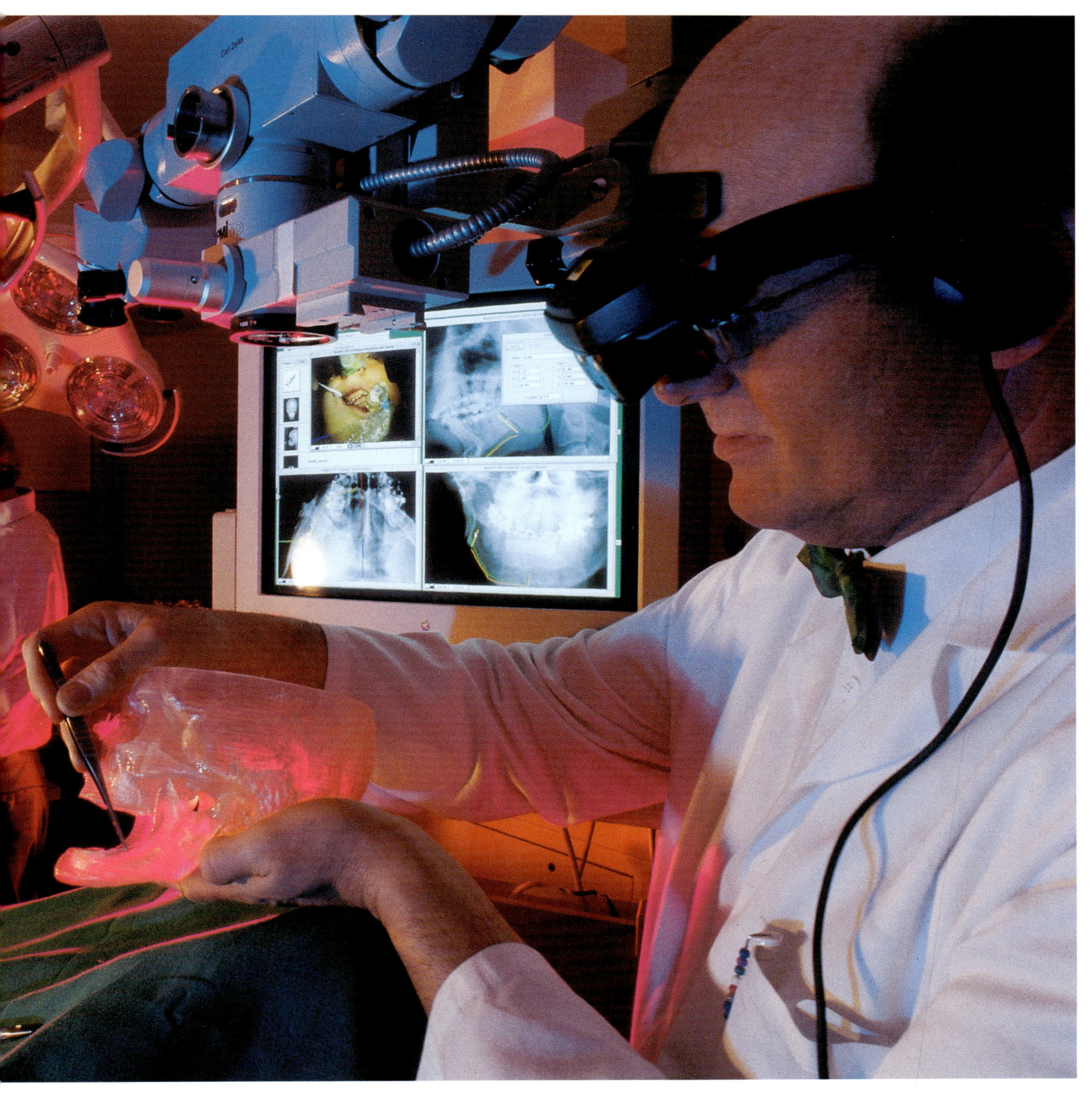

Viennese medicine is still world famous even 100 years after Billroth. Above: the General Hospital,
Department for Oral and Facial Surgery, Prof. Rolf Ewers performs VDU-assisted oral surgery.
Opposite: the Social Medical Centre East (Donauspital), a connecting corridor in the basement.

CHRISTKINDLMARKT

The market named for the Christ child –
Where many felled firs lay
Was a Viennese world of stalls high piled
Along the Paradise way.

Silvery serpents fluttered free,
The nuts were ripening slowly.
The crib stood there in mystery,
Tiny, bright and holy.

The fresh snow lay crisp as they peered,
And mist hung all around,
As if plucked from St Nicholas' beard –
No footfall heard, no sound.

To Jewish children, Bethlehem
Brought no shy sense of danger,
For in that stable one of them
Was lying in the manger.

BERTHOLD VIERTEL

Preceding pages: the view from the Burgtheater to the square in front of the City Hall – films are shown here on huge screens during the summer months. Opposite and above: this square also features popular entertainment in the winter months: the "Eistraum" offers healthy outdoor entertainment in spectacular surroundings.

Preceding pages: Legislative sessions are dignified by antique Grecian décor: The Parliament Building
was erected by Theophil Hansen in 1874–1883 and is one of the most distinctive of the
Ringstrasse buildings. Above: the former Conference Hall of the Reichsratssitzungssaal.
Opposite: the head of the statue of Pallas Athena in front of the Parliament.

PARLIAMENT

The Parliament is high and wide
could be described as spacious
and at its doors
they award the symbol of membership

This is broad and round
and is given to the member
who is busy

With human duty
the members are
lingering in their idleness

Parliament looks after the
members
and they get their pay
by signing for it.

EDMUND MACH

THE TRAFFIC

Someone asked what the crossing keeper posted at a Vienna street crossing was actually supposed to be doing. And, because no one seemed able to give an answer, he provided his own: "He's there to make sure he doesn't get run over!" But in Vienna every good joke is bad as soon as it's made: there is no conceivable exaggeration you could come up with here that will not have been outdone by the facts within the hour. The crossing keeper had been warned. But he wouldn't listen, and sure enough he paid the price. He was standing there controlling the traffic, and he was run over. Wherever you go in Vienna, the external things of life cause problems. If, today, you wanted to paint a picture entitled "The Bad Old Days" you'd have to paint a cab rank with a few pensively seated figures. The siesta of obstructed traffic. And then, if you wanted to show the new age, you would depict a scene showing the crossing keeper, hand still raised imploringly, being hit by the car. The driver is a fiend incarnate, no doubt of that. But what road racer might not, one day, be tempted by the urge to run over Vienna's traffic population? Perhaps even the trams here feel a strange compulsion to ram buses? Just as it may be true that the road surfaces of Naples are smoother than the tram rails of the Ring, so it is hard to see the disasters of this city, failures even at the planning stage, as anything but the work of the knockabout clowns, whose idea of regulating social intercourse is to beat each other over the head.

KARL KRAUS

Above and opposite: the fiaker or hackney cab is an anachronistic, but nevertheless popular form of transport – it is ecologically correct and not much slower than a car in the traffic congestion of a large city.

VIENNA

Vienna: city with sleeve guards
where they ride the T-line tram
to St Marx
a cake shop
full of Johann Strausses
lures an onion-
patterned recruit
to abandon his sampler crocheting
in the barracks
and become a cake icer
lavender-coloured
smelling of violets and
mothballs
Europe's spoilt child
of the Balkans kisses
in many languages
(e.g.)
your hand.

ELFRIEDE GERSTL

72

The city of music likes to present itself in all its finery. Above: the view from the Albertina Ramp
to the Staatsoper with the equestrian statue of Archduke Albrecht to the right.
Opposite above: the foyer of the Staatsoper. Below: a frontal view of the Staatsoper as seen from the Ringstrasse.

THE MASK
OF BEETHOVEN

Beethoven makes a very popular decoration. Like a china plate, a set of antlers or one of those samplers with "Bless this house" stitched on it. Beethoven is an international staple of interior decoration, who goes well with any set of opinions displayed on the wall. With Lueger and Marx, with the nutcracker visage of the General and the lofty brow of the worthy Rabbi Moses ben Maimon, and the militant-melancholy Polish moustache of the revaluer of all values.

He looks best, of course, above the piano. But he is also quite happy at the head of the bed, and even if banished to the top of the hall cupboard, where the bottled fruit goes, he raises the intellectual tone of the premises.

The cunning housewife with a damp patch on the wall will prefer a relatively large-sized Beethoven. Like that famous picture of the maestro seated at the piano, surrounded by a circle of adoring listeners. One of them in particular – arms locked around his drawn-up knees, chin resting on them – is ostentatiously listening with his very soul. This picture, too, is a popular choice: the head of Beethoven with a pair of naked lovers nestling in the forest of his hair. A rare species of louse – Pediculus capitis Beeth.

But more popular than any of these pictures –

Once a year the Opera is thrown open for festivities; Vienna's Opera Ball is the social event of the season.
Preceding pages: "Alles Walzer!" is the traditional call that turns the floor over to the public.
Above: the opening polonaise. Opposite, above and below: view towards the stalls.

even the one where Beethoven the democrat keeps the courtier Goethe waiting at Karlsbad, or the one where he goes stumbling through Döbling with coat-tails flying and you can actually see that he's just had the idea for the Eroica – more popular than all these as a wall decoration is the mask of Beethoven, the plaster copy of his face moulded by the sculptor Franz Klein in 1812 (and often wrongly referred to as a death mask).

How many hundreds of thousands of pianos worldwide stand below that gloomy countenance, defenceless against the Pathétique sonata ("With feeling, Melanie, with feeling!") and the onslaughts of a four-handed duet that makes symphonies moan with pain and overtures disintegrate. The most extraordinary features that God's stylus ever scribed, a helpless victim of women and popularity!

What playwright would ever forget to specify the mask of Beethoven over the piano? In the heraldic devices of concert agencies that fearful brow broods, pressed into service as the logo of instrument makers, stamped in leather on music cases, hacked into the wood of music stands, printed in the bookplates of operetta libretti, used as a trade mark for rosin, piano candles, ear trumpets, bird whistles and automatic pianolas.

Why not a Beethoven masked ball to celebrate the hundred and fiftieth anniversary of the day on which the master's eyes first opened on the darkness of this world?

Art is serious, life's a jest.

And even more of a jest after death – immortality.

ALFRED POLGAR

Vienna is the city of music. Opposite: the most famous conductors have conducted and the best orchestras played in the Golden Hall of the Vienna Musikverein whose acoustics are unique. Above left: a performance of the Wiener Konzertquintett in the Sala Terrena of the House of the Teutonic Knights in Singerstrasse.
Above right: an open-air performance of "The Magic Flute" at the Roman Ruins in the park of Schönbrunn Palace.

MONUMENT

In Vienna's Stadtpark stands, silent and cold, a little man wearing a little coat of gold.

And not just his little coat is golden. His boots are golden too, and his trousers, his face, his moustache, his wavy hair, his eyes, his ears, his hands. The whole man is golden, top to toe. He has a golden violin tucked under his golden chin, and his golden fingers hold a golden bow. The golden man is Johann Strauss, who distilled the most elegant and fragrant musical essence from the popular air of Vienna. There he stands, to the life. He was that tall and that slender, he wore his moustache like that and his hair was waved like that. Everything that was transient about him, fixed in time and external, has been captured and defined in his monument.

Above and opposite: the bronze monument for Johann Strauss in the Stadtpark, which was already planned in 1904 but only unveiled in 1921, has been gleaming in golden lustre for some years now.

Preceding pages: the Mozart Monument by Victor Tilgner in the Burggarten reflects the legend of gilded youth. Tourism, too, is eager to capitalise on the perennial appeal of Mozart. Above: Otmar Lang, violin maker to the Vienna Philharmonic and the Staatsoper, in his atelier for making and repairing violins. Opposite: "Anyone who lives continuously in a city of music is glad when the season ends, because all the unmusical people leave and there is more time left for finger work". (Ingeborg Bachmann)

When you look at the monument there are many things that come to mind, not just the music of Strauss. But when you listen to the music of Strauss, the monument inevitably comes to mind. An unfortunate consequence of love cast in bronze.

ALFRED POLGAR

Traditional and high quality Viennese craftsmanship.
Above: the workshop of the glass firm Lobmeyr, former "royal and imperial court
glazier and court glassware dealer", a lampmaker creating a chandelier.
Above right: Elisabeth Krebs' workshop for metal restoration.
Below right: an exquisite pattern being engraved at Lobmeyr.

o fair vienna, built on zilk!

vienna is where the zilk grazes.

every viennese has his zilk!

zilk gazes deep into the viennese heart.

deep gazes the zilk into the viennese heart.

ERNST JANDL

COURTESY

Good morning! Minus eleven degrees. Those who now
are out and about are red-nosed with the cold.
Even so: good morning!
Day promises to come again. The chimneys
are cowled with birds. Day is coming.
A day of circlets lying
On snow-heaped roofs of cars.
O cold future. In the next moment,
on the Prater's big wheel blocks of ice
wobble through the air. And penguins
crouch inside and say Ah
in Japanese. Good morning!
Minus eleven degrees. And now, for our
early risers and pets: the Blue Danube.
Good morning, allahu ekber.

LUDWIG FELS

Bird's-eye-views: above the view from the tower of the City Hall across the city with the Burgtheater in the foreground. Left: the classical Theseus Temple in the Volksgarten.

THE STEPHANSDOM

The Stephansdom is more than just a Noah's Ark in stone, in which traces and symbols of Vienna's history have ridden out the flood of the ages. It is also an example of "the faith that moves mountains". Initially, blocks of a marine sandstone known as muschelkalk were quarried, mainly from the Leitha mountains, and brought to Vienna. Masons and master-builders then set to work to reassemble the mountain in new, geometrical shapes – to give it a crystalline form, as it were. First and foremost, then, this cathedral is part of the natural world. The materials from which it was built include fossils, such as oyster shells, and calcite crystals formed from the disintegrated shells of sea urchins. "Second-hand" building materials were also used –

stone from the outer wall of the Roman camp of Vindobona and Roman burial slabs. Clearly, the builders had no time for squeamishness. The Christian religion had a preference for building its churches on former sites of what it called "heathen" worship, to wipe out traces of other religions. The "Roman" blocks in the ca-

Above and left: the design of the neo-Baroque Michaelerkuppel echoes the imposing Baroque building of the Karlskirche (St. Charles' Church) on Karlsplatz, which was built by the Fischer von Erlachs (both father and son) between 1716 and 1737.

St. Stephen's Cathedral is the national shrine of Austria, and its reconstruction after the war was a patriotic concern that involved all other federal provinces alongside Vienna itself. Preceding pages: the "Pummerin", the largest bell in Austria, hangs in the north tower and – apart from New Year's Eve – is only rung on special occasions. Above: "It can't be pointed out too often that we have the most solemn church interior in the whole of Christendom" (Adolf Loos). A view through the nave of St. Stephen's Cathedral towards the high altar. Opposite, above: the Church of the Minorites with its starkly simple forms contrasts with the Gothic and Baroque splendour of other Viennese places of worship. Opposite below left and right: Maria am Gestade and Vienna's oldest church, St. Ruprecht's.

...thedral are the first traces of human endeav-
our in this Ark of stone; together with other
traces, often less easy to interpret, they form a
fragmented conceptual construct that caused
the cathedral to become the symbol of Austria
as a whole. It is primarily a monument to
Habsburg Catholicism – sometimes more
Habsburg than Catholic, sometimes vice-
versa. The historical graffiti of which this conceptual construct consists are also scratched
into the minds and consciousness of the Austrian people, often without their being in
the least aware of the fact. So a study of the
Stephansdom is also the study of an Austrian
mind and the memory that resides there, and
the attitudes which that memory consciously
or unconsciously dictates. (...)

Until the year 1683, when the Turks laid siege
to Vienna for the second time, the spire bore
the sun and crescent emblems of Papacy and
Empire, serving even then as a symbol of the

unity of church and state, Catholic Church and Habsburg "Emperors by the grace of God".

A glance into the stonemasons' yard of history reveals the traumas of Austria, the first and greatest of which was the threat posed by the Turks to the spiritual supremacy of the Catholic church and the temporal dominion of the Habsburgs. "Türkenpoldl", "Little Turkeypoldl", as the Emperor Leopold I was later nicknamed, fled the city during this second siege, taking refuge first at Passau and later at Linz. During this period the Stephansdom was struck by over a thousand cannonballs. The roof was constantly being "made good"

with tarpaulins, to create the impression that the city had plenty of material resources available. Even today, cannonballs are still walled into the masonry of the south tower and the nave, souvenirs of the coming of the Turks.

Above and opposite page: this is where Franz Schubert played the organ – the parish church of Lichtental.

Non-Christian religions also have their places of worship in Vienna.
Above: the Peace Stupa at Handelskai was built by private subscription – Austria was
the first country in Europe to officially recognise Buddhism. Right: the Islamic Centre at
Bruckhaufen was opened in 1979 and houses two mosques, a Koran school and an assembly hall.

When the legendary Polish King Jan Sobiesky had driven off the Turks, another legendary figure in Austrian history, Prince Eugene, defeated the Turkish Grand Vizier Kara Mustapha in nine battles, and in doing so laid the foundations of the Danube monarchy. As is only natural, this great general too lies buried in the Stephansdom.

GERHARD ROTH

SEEGASSE

Noah's Ark passed by on the canal. The Negro watching his commanding officer's car outside the barbed wire saw it. He recognised it by the white goose sitting on top and beating its wings, but he said nothing.

The little balls still bounce on the flat roof, but the old woman who used to lie in bed by the window is no longer there. Who are we to tell that we are living under a new order? The street leading to the water is empty.

The bees gather on the bank, seeking their last queen.

ILSE AICHINGER

Above and left: the Jewish Congregation in Vienna worships in the synagogue in the Seitenstettengasse (First District). Overleaf: there are a number of very old gravestones in the Jewish cemetery in the Seegasse, some of which date back to the 13th century.

A WIENERLIED OF THE GRAVES

As a child
Holding my grandfather's hand
I was often led
Through Vienna's cemeteries:
Central cemetery,
71st terminus
And evangelical churchyard,
Matzleinsdorfer Platz,
I remember especially well:
Three generations lie scattered there –
Catholic craftsmen,
Evangelical housewives,
Jewish doctors …
They'd be amazed
That I'd find no peace near them,
Although that should play no part
In the sense
Of Eternal Rest
Which knows no frontiers –
And, consequently,
No geographical location either!

All Saints and All Souls
Daisies brightly rain down,
Through rustling foliage,
Knee-deep,
Drum-roll of a mass for the dead
Of which a child knows nothing …!

WOLFGANG GEORG FISCHER

*"Everyone who dies in Austria has the right to a halo" (Gerhard Roth). The Zentralfriedhof
(Central Cemetery) is a vast necropolis and a world unto itself that has often been celebrated in poetry and song;
it is also a focal point of Viennese identity. Above: the tomb of honour of the furniture manufacturer Michael Thonet.
Opposite: Adolf Loos' grave of honour provides welcome relief to pseudo-historical pomp.*

Preceding pages: a wonderful view of the Danube may be had from Kahlenbergerdorf cemetery.
Above: every year in November a raft decorated by flowers is launched in the harbour at Albern beside
the Friedhof der Namenlosen ("Cemetery of the Nameless") to commemorate the victims of the Danube.
Below: the six large anti-aircraft bunkers are a reminder of the closing phase
of the Second World War; this picture shows the bunker in the Augarten Park.
Opposite: Vienna's animal cemetery in Sierndorf near Stockerau.

DOD EN WOSSA

waun s me aussezan
waun s me aussezan
aus da donau
untan wintahofm
bei oewan
wiad ma des monogram
wos ma mei muta r amoe
en s hemt zeichnt hod
lenxt fawoschn sei:
a monogramdintn
is aa nua r a mendsch
und hoet ned ewech …

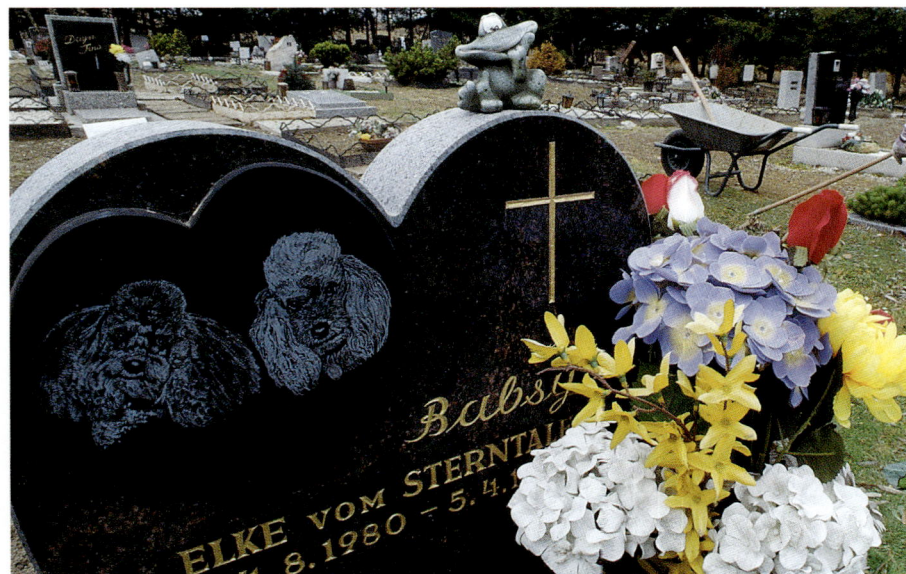

waun s me aussezan
waun s me aussezan
untan wintahofm
bei oewan
en heabst
how e a neix monogram
a leichz und a schweas
wäu s me amoe auffedrad hod
und amoe owe aum grund
und hii und hea
wia s en wossa scho is ..
und da suma woa laung
und de schdrömung ned schdoak
und de wassreche gengd
hod es iwreche gmocht ..

a fisch fia de wön
und a r aunka fia n grund
oes monogram unta d aung
is bessa r oes kans –
owa drozzdem ka easoz
fia des schene blaue
wos ma mei muta seinazeid
en s hemad einezeichnt
hod ..

waun s me aussezan
waun s me aussezan
en heabst
bei oewan
untan wintahofm …

H.C. ARTMANN

The Danube has only a marginal effect on the cityscape: there are only two (albeit heavily populated) districts on the far side of the river. But this is where the New Vienna is unfolding and spreading into the surrounding plain. Above: the view from the Leopoldsberg to the Danube and Danube Island. Opposite: angler on the banks of the New Danube.

The Danube is a recreational paradise. Preceding pages: the "Copa Kagrana" on the Danube Island (called after a district on the other side of the Danube) and its numerous bars attract hordes of pleasure seekers, especially on balmy summer evenings. The Leopoldsberg can be seen in the background. Above: Schneider Boat Rentals on the Old Danube. Opposite below: garden allotments, like those in "Auf der Schmelz" in the 15th District, also are a part the Viennese way of life.

ALONG THE DANUBE

Along the Danube
the thoughts come
like fish and children.

Along the Danube the
doubts come;
Freud, Schönberg, dreams
and music,
memories – illusion and its
meaning,
hands on the unruly strings of the zither
and grey coats in the rain,
moustaches below spiked helmets.

Along the Danube evening soon falls,
but when the sun rises above the river
it brings an armistice,
between understanding and madness,
between harmony and discord,
between guns and roses.

Along the Danube the course of history often
loses its balance.
But when it regains it again
Our eyes look on
beyond the river's banks
toward a European destiny
intent on survival –

GASTONE BIGGI

A LITTLE TOPOGRAPHY
OF REDISCOVERY

I.
First we went home
to the servant madonna.
We had no need to tell her
anything, she already knew it all
and smiled, tender and loving,
more beautiful than ever before.

II.
In Domgasse we stopped trying to count
the lovers' kisses that,
in evening stillness, flowered
on their lips and cheeks.

Opposite: one can bathe in great style in the Amalienbad at Reumannplatz.
Above left: the timetable in an old-fashioned bathhouse in Hermanngasse.
Above right: the Engel Apotheke, in pure Art Nouveau style, in Bognergasse, First District.

DER · ZEIT · IHRE · KVNST ·
ER · KVNST · IHRE · FREIHEI

III.

In Blutgasse dark had already fallen.
It smelt warmly and sweetly
of vanilla and butter cake.
You grasped my hand and asked,
"Is this the home of the Wienerwald witch,
baking so seductively?"
And I said only, "Run, Hänsel, run!"

IV.

We were still too excited
to let the Ancora Verde detain us.
But at the Alte Schmiede
we went down into the cellar
of our remembered past.
In red wine's fires
what had been shattered fused
back together. And our hearts' beatings
Found a new synchrony.

CHRISTINE BUSTA

*Opposite: the Viennese have long since become used
to the once wildly controversial figurehead (it was denounced
as a "Assyrian privy") of Art Nouveau movement, the Secession
building, with its characteristic dome of gilt laurel leaves.
Above: a Stadtbahn (today Underground) Station by
Otto Wagner, with the Musikverein Building in the background.*

THE FADING OF VIENNA

Vienna bravely faced the besieging Turks.
Twice they defended themselves and then
the battle was won at Aspern.
Vienna at the turn of the century
was full of dancing, various balls were held.
Strauss struck up and different couples
spun across the floor.
Life and its living were
especially beautiful.
People trusted and hoped that the good
life would continue and was continuing.
Sometimes melodies were heard, some-
times there was singing in the streets.
Sometimes they danced in the Domeyer

and out in Favoriten.
All in all, it was a lovely fading of
Vienna.

EDMUND MACH

120

Otto Wagner was the most prominent architect of fin de siècle Vienna and many of his buildings still dominate the cityscape (e.g. the Stadtbahn viaducts). Above: the apartment houses in Linke Wienzeile 38 and 40 belong to the icons of the Art Nouveau style. Opposite: detail of the Steinhof Church.

The turn of the century was a golden age for Vienna. Above: a decorative figure on the roof of the Postsparkasse building which was erected by Otto Wagner between 1904 and 1907. Opposite above: the entrance front of the Postsparkasse building seen from Georg-Coch-Platz. Opposite below: detail of the façade of the "Loos House" in Michaelerplatz. Overleaf: the restorer Stöbe at work on Gustav Klimt's "Beethoven Frieze" in the Secession.

A LANDSCAPE
FOR ANGELS

Then I discovered, with some prompting from my grandmother, Karoline Scholdan, the uppermost classes. "They're nothing but a bunch of enchanted rogues" said my grandmother. That they were. The attic storeys of innumerable buildings were their territory. Saints and lemurs, centaurs and atlases, with fossilised plumage and metallic knots of vipers. Seemingly ready to swoop down at any moment, or fly away, or just sunk in their own thoughts. Smilingly carrying the weight of the firmament or warding it off with trepidation. Showing comets their way. Lay-bys for sparrows, crows and pigeons. Proud wind vanes in midst of swathes of soot and smoke. A masked ball of the most fanciful kind. Undoubtedly my kind of people! And because they were enchanted, I wanted to be enchanted, too. Sometimes, and I'm absolutely sure of this, the spell was broken, and the petrified and stiff limbs loosened into movement and airiness. Then these creatures amused each other by recounting their observations, while dancing the whole time to the strains of a music that can only be heard by those who know where to seek the Viennese God.

ANDRÉ HELLER

Visitors to the Kunsthistorisches Museum can relax after viewing the collection in the café.
Opposite, above: the fourth largest art collection in the world contains many
masterpieces, especially of Spanish, Dutch, Italian and French painting.

THE PAST

The past has to tower up before us, like rampantly proliferating vegetation, virtually in a state of tumescence. The disavowal which has been imposed on it later, at the dress-rehearsal stage, like a carnival hat, has nothing whatever to do with its existence as present, and existed at that time merely as a possibility, which only now seems to be an inevitable reality that, in his rigidified form, obstructs our view of the entirely plastic condition in which it existed at the time.

HEIMITO VON DODERER

A copyist in the Bruegel Room of the Kunsthistorisches Museum.
Opposite, above: the Egyptian and Oriental Collection ranges from Egyptian culture to
the early Christian period. Opposite, below: the museum building is also utilised for other
cultural events, e.g. the rehearsal of a concert of the Jeunesse Musicale.

RELEARNING VIENNA

I cling to this city, how I cling to this city, why
do I cling to this city, is it because I was born
here, have always lived here, because I lit all
my candles here, because I followed or had to
follow unfathomable decisions, I cling to this
city but I don't love it, I've become used to it,
it's familiar to me, I'm familiar in it, I entrust
myself to it, I am at peace in myself when I
am here and beside myself
and lost to myself when I am
not here, I am at rest in it, I
trust it and I trust in it to
keep me as it always has kept
me, so I want to be at rest
here later when I cannot,
may not, continue living. I
love living in this city, but I

Above: the Collection of Arms and Armour of the Kunsthistorisches Museum in the Hofburg.
Opposite, above: the Ephesos Museum in the Hofburg with the statue of Artemis.
Opposite, below: visitors ascending the splendid staircase of the Kunsthistorisches are
confronted by Antonio Canova's sculptural group in marble, "Theseus Combating the Centaur".

do not love this city, it is largely a matter of indifference to me. Nor do I love its inhabitants, but I am used to them, they are basically a matter of indifference to me as long as they leave me alone, as long as they do not fall upon me and tear me to pieces. Sometimes they disgust me, just as I sometimes disgust myself, sometimes this city disgusts me, nausea, queasiness, vomiting overcome me, hydrants become zebras! But the next moment I am reconciled again, to myself, to the city, to the inhabitants. Sometimes something happens, something bright, I don't know, there are these glittering moments, at sunset, in the twilight, a gentle shadow over the rooftops, a gleaming church pinnacle, the end of an old long beautiful street converging to a distant dot, I look up to the top of St Stephen's and down again to its foundations, always up and down, it makes me giddy, I should like to go on living. Or my eye traces the outlines of the towers, domes and hills on the western horizon, I stand at the window of my home, wearing my suit of lights. If anyone asks me what keeps me here I say that everything keeps me here, even what is ugly. Even the memories, meagre now. Of my childhood, of my parents, of the life and death of my father, my grandparents, my friends and companions, now the mind's eye flourishes. I have fought for every tree, in the wide courtyard opposite me there were once three chestnut trees and two oaks, radiant in spring, I want to take better care of the last, but the most beautiful streets have

The Naturhistorisches Museum, which is a fascinating example of the museum culture of the yesteryear.

now been disguised, I think they have gone right downhill, have become decayed regions of clamour and filth and have lost all their charm, so I no longer understand anything at all, the calendar is fraying, my heartfelt wish. Vienna means something to me, and I no longer think about that, on a winter day my shadow lies long in front of me and I ask my shadow where it's going, where are you going I ask my shadow, where do you have to get to, I walk in fear in Vienna says the shadow, I leave the sun behind me, I am afraid but I run away from it in Vienna, I always run away from it but I stay in Vienna, I can only be

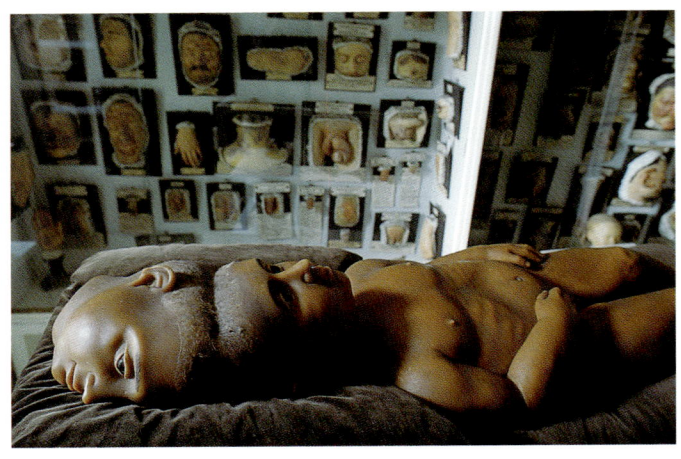

here, even with the fear. Then the fear becomes the written record of my thoughts, the more fear the more writing, sometimes I fly, the sky is at its most beautiful here.

FRIEDERIKE MAYRÖCKER

This is where Dr. Freud revealed the secrets of the human soul: his former consulting rooms at Berggasse 19 are now a museum.
Opposite, above: the Pathological Anatomical Federal Museum is housed in the "Narrenturm"
("Bedlam") in the Old General Hospital and is the oldest and largest of its kind in the world.
Opposite, below: the "Venus Medici" is a particular elegant specimen from the collection
of anatomical wax figures housed in the Institute for Medical History.

VIENNESE POISON

I love this sultrily enervating, deceptively confusing, characterless and corrupt city, this grubby and pompous Vienna, gorged and drunk on its own past, reduced to prostituting itself as a mouldering museum. This city, which has no respect for what is venerable and makes no stand against vulgarity, but treats both the same, beholding and bemoaning and then dismissing with a jest. I cling to this city, and I love it with hate and with tenderness, with dread and with laughter, and with a cool, objective sadness that is not without a hint of frivolity.

INGE MERKEL

The Austrian Gallery in the Upper Belvedere displays art ranging from the 19th to the early 20th century, including famous works by Egon Schiele and Gustav Klimt. Above: the "Crouching Figure" (1900/01) by May Klinger is in the foreground, with "The Violet Hat" (1909) by Gustav Klimt in the background. Opposite: the Schiele Room.

CELESTIAL PHENOMENA

It happens sometimes in Vienna that a south wind gets up during the night. When it does, it keeps blowing steadily all day through the city streets. It makes it hard to breathe. Because, mixed with the dust of the city, reddish sand from the coasts of the Gulf of Sidra penetrates the respiratory system, causing coughing, heart murmurs and headaches.

In the afternoon these inconvenient symptoms ease. The sky turns green and limpid as water. High above, the clouds drift lazily. Distant mountain ranges with blue-shadowed valleys and wide beaches tower up in a strangely glistening light. Then a sudden movement in the atmosphere breaks up and shifts the thrusting mass of clouds, which for a few seconds takes on the exact mirror image of the island patterns of the Aegean. The whole archipelago rides up there like a giant map, on a sky as glass-clear as the midday surface of the sea.

At the very moment when this aerial vision has achieved its maximum purity and geographical precision, it is suddenly distorted. The wind dies away and the magical light is extinguished. Streaky structures of cloud swiftly draw a veil over the illusion.

Once every twenty years or so this curious phenomenon can be seen in Vienna, the best view being above the city centre.

INGE MERKEL

Preceding pages: a sphinx in the park of Belvedere Palace. Opposite the Upper Belvedere. Above: the Lower Belvedere. Below: the Palace of Prince Eugene as ornamentation – a panorama plate with the Belvedere as motif from the Imperial Silver Collection.

Above: it was above all Maria Theresia and Franz Joseph I, perhaps the two most popular Habsburgs,
who left their mark on Schönbrunn Palace and Park. Thousands of tourists follow their trail every day.
Opposite: the monument to Maria Theresia.

SCHEMBRUN

waun e noch schembrun gee
ge r e bein haubtdoa r eine
und omad bein maxingdial
ge r e wida r ausse ..

schembrun:
bein haubtdoa r eine
schembrun:
bein maxingdial wida r ausse
schembrun ..

en früjoa scheint d sun
und da mond
und de schdean

waun e in s boemanhaus kum
schdüü i da r a boa bluman!

schembrun ..

en suma rengd s olawäu nua
waun s ned soi –
en diagoatn schaun d ölefauntn
med eanare aung en d woikn ..

schembrun ..

Above: the Great Gallery in Schönbrunn is the architectural focal point of the palace.
Opposite: The Equestrian Room, placed between one of the Chinese Cabinets
and the Hall of Ceremonies with the so-called Marshal's Table.

en heabst is da himö blau
und de blaln schleiffm umadum

waun e endlech duat drom
bein maxingdial wida r aussekum
daun muas e linx ume iwa d maua!

schembrun ..

bein eigaung unt
schrein en naboleaun seine goidan odla
bein ausgangl om owa
is nua mea da fridhof
met de fün liachtaln ..

H. C. ARTMANN

Above: the ornamental fountains in front of the palace. Right: the view from the park of Schönbrunn Palace towards the Gloriette. Opposite: the Wagenburg houses a collection of historic carriages and coaches.

LEOPOLDSTADT DANCING SONG

I feel like somersaulting in the winter meadows
Parliaments of ducks on the thin ice at Heustadel
Bare mistletoe in the trees at Jesuitenwiese
I've got this urge to take bites out of the air.

With what teeth in what cold winters?
I don't put the question. I want to swap
Ice kisses with my girl and race round the pavilion
I have such a desire for a royal fall of snow.

That is what gives me pleasure in myself:
that kind of pleasure,
A down-to-earth Viennese, a mist on Rustenschach avenue,
A Schüttelstrasse wind with cradled Orion
Looking down on the Simmering country.

In these bitter cold inner winters
While I am alone, and it rains pennies,
In my dreams the desire becomes quite mad
And the wind bites back. Matters not to me.

Along the central avenue my old friend limps
The Carinthian Slav from Kagrania
And wants the simple life while painting pictures.

I hop beside him, till at half-past four the crows
Sweep the sky clean
Before they go to roost.

Then I'll dance reels and the horse chestnuts
Frame the evening light in their swaying tops.
I've had enough pleasure, and now the frosts are going.

ROBERT SCHINDEL

Above: a hay wagon belonging to the Municipality of Vienna, Department for Forestry and Agricultural Enterprises. Opposite: "Ich schnitt' es gern in alle Rinden ein" (Schubert's "Die schöne Müllerin"): tree carvings in the Vienna Woods.

149

There are two Praters – which is the most attractive is a matter of personal taste.
Above: fair day of the Croats from Burgenland in the Bohemian Prater on the Laaerberg.
Opposite: scenes from the "real" Prater, a roller coaster and the Giant Ferris Wheel, a fire-eater
and a try-your-strength machine with a strongman of wood.

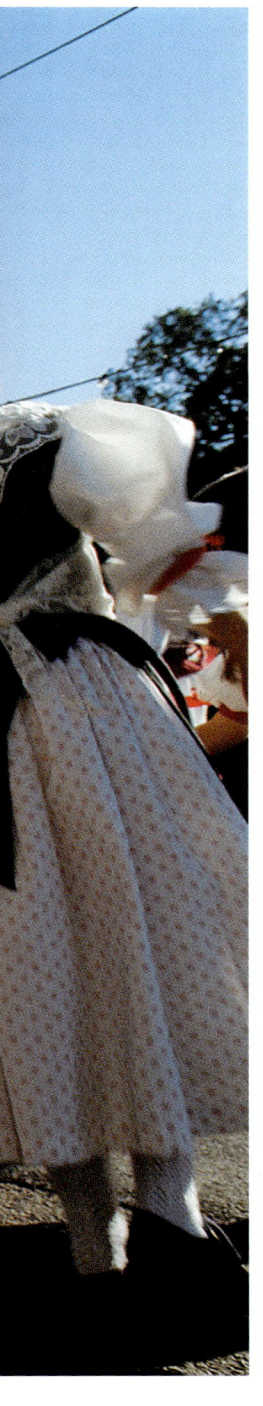

CHESTNUT

The main avenue of the Prater is the domain of the chestnut tree, Aesculus hippocastanum in Latin, horse chestnut in the vernacular. Not so much a domain as a dictatorship. Although its true home is in the mountains of northern Greece, it has long since acquired botanical squatter's rights here. It is the tree that stands for Vienna: its blossom is red and white, its fruit is encased in a soft-spiked shell, is inedible and looks like an offcut from a piece of polished mahogany furniture. If the horse chestnut were not so common, it would be very uncommon indeed. Had it not become so widespread, you would pay good money to go and look at it. Year after year it suffers the fate of a tune heard once too often: an unstoppable descent from originality into

banality. When the opening bud extends the first spray of blossom, the grateful heart feels like bursting into a hymn of delight. A few months later it feels more like weeping to see how commonplace the massed magic has become, the white insipid and the red coarse. Muzak for the eye.

It blossoms in May along both sides of the main avenue: Aesculus hippocastanum.

In August, just a horse chestnut.

ALFRED POLGAR

Above a detail of the Giant Ferris Wheel.
Opposite: a tribune belonging to the race course at Freudenau.

Vienna and wine: a never-ending story. Above: wine harvest on the Wilhelminenberg.
Opposite, above: wine tasting in the cellars of Stammersdorf.
Opposite, below: Schlumberger's cellars for sparkling wine.
Overleaf: vineyards near Ried Alsegg on the small Schafberg.

THE TRUE AND THE FALSE HEURIGE

When a foreigner comes to Vienna for the first time and asks for information about those local pleasures and cultural peculiarities which do not appear in any travel guide, he will be asked ninety-nine times out of a hundred:

"Have you been to a Heurige (wine garden) yet? You simply must go to one! To Grinzing, Liebhartstal, Sievering or up to the Hohe Warte."

Upon which the man's experiences begin: He is pushed into a car, which stops after a

quarter of an hour in front of the broad entrance of a street-level house, under the gable of which, dangling at the end of a broom handle sticking out into the street, is a small part of a branch of yellowing fir – the symbol of the Heurige. A long line of cars stand quietly forgotten, their drivers have also gone in. Jollity pounces on him in the entrance hall; as here mostly lie those hidden places, where cheerfulness finds its release; strange giants stomp in pairs over the courtyard, steam coming from their mouths and glassy eyed, while three women talk into a closed wooden door. In the background something musical is

Left: the "Lichtentaler Quartett" playing at the Heurige Ortner in Ottakring. Below: Heuriger in Oberlaa. Opposite: it would be more prudent to descend the "Hirnbrecherstiege" ("skull-breaking steps") in Kahlenbergerdorf while still sober.

Austria's capital also has a great deal to offer gourmets. Above: Helmut Österreicher and his team at the restaurant "Steiereck" serve haute cuisine. Below: this was a favourite dish of Emperor Franz Joseph – a tafelspitz in the restaurant Plachutta.

bubbling away, a mixture of rumbling, singing and scraping. The claws reach out for the newcomer and pull him towards them.

He steps into an elongated low-ceilinged room, a village pub the size of a dancefloor; the tables are long, roughly built, no tablecloth, benches run along either side. The air at blood-heat from fumes which are a mixture of sounds and smells: tobacco, accordi-

Above: Artists as well as the publican and the cooks enjoy their meals together in the "Schnattl" in the Josefstadt.
Below: A Schnitzel hanging over the "edge of the plate like a Fellini cleavage" (Alfred Komarek)
can be enjoyed at the restaurant "Zu den zwei Liserln".

on, rough alcohol, laughter, whispering, wine and song. Garlands and Chinese lanterns hang from the ceiling - obviously in order that the guest is not simply catered for acoustically and aromatically, but optically as well.

The atmosphere is peaceful but loud: the young men with smart buttonholes, who at the side of rosy-cheeked girls (both parties look suspiciously like they belong in the

Although the notoriously coarse Naschmarkt women have largely disappeared, the overwhelming culinary choice remains. Above and opposite, above: vegetable and sausage stands in the Naschmarkt. Opposite, below: a kosher butcher in the Leopoldstadt.

reception room at a lawyer's office) intone a delightful "nonsense" song, would not be out of place at a lads' bar; the correct faces, which now, wearing a little jester's hat, suggest an obliviousness to the outside world, do not look encouraging; their inebriation has the premeditation of northern zones. Otherwise, of course, the social mix seems to be provided for; as between every two refined guests (whose car is waiting outside) sits a quiet minion or cobbler's mate gazing round in satisfaction.

ANTON KUH

COFFEEHOUSE

An important figure in the coffee-houses was and still is the headwaiter. He is always addressed as "Herr" and then his first name. Coffee-house waiters are of a different style than those in other gastronomic establishments; their age for a start, which as a rule is around fifty.

The coffee-house requires mirrors on the wall, crystal chandeliers hanging from the ceiling, which are also on during the day, tables with tops of real or imitation marble are the

Contemplation, introspection and conviviality: the coffee-house is a way of life.
Above and opposite page: Café Schopenhauer in the 18th District.
Opposite, above: the café in the Museum for Applied Art.

A very luxurious way of gaining a few calories.
Above: the only real and genuine original Sachertorte
is served in the Café Sacher.
Opposite, above: the Imperial Saloon in Demel's Patisserie.
Opposite, below: Café Landtmann.

norm, plush sofas, wooden chairs and in the middle of the room is the cakes buffet. The rest of the food on offer is rather modest.

The very first coffee-houses attracted their clientele with the gazettes available. Today proper Viennese cafés offer all of the Austrian newspapers plus a large part of the other German language and a few selected international broadsheets.

The coffee drunk there is strong. The basic is der grosse Schwarze, a large black coffee, which is a Mocca, and which can be turned into a Braunen, white coffee, or Einspänner, Viennese speciality, with the addition of milk or cream (in the Viennese dialect, Obers). There are a multitude of variations, some of which are the speciality of a particular coffee-house. With each cup, known in Vienna as a Schale, a glass of water will also be served across the top of which a small coffee-spoon will be lying.

ROLF SCHNEIDER

NORDBAHNSTRASSEN-BLUES

i walk down nordbahnstrasse walking the number 5 line
i smoke cigarettes a few drags hand casually in pocket
i whistle and spit the butt out in front of me
the air's hot and even hotter in the pub i order a shot of rye

Vienna's night life has shaken off the lethargy that often characterised it in the past.
Above: in the Loos Bar. Opposite, above: the "Dennstedt".
Opposite, below: "First Floor".

i walk down nordbahnstrasse walking the number 5 line
the air's hot and even hotter in the pub i order a shot of rye
and the white-lead breast of a tart
i feed the machine and see the landlady's glazed eyes

i walk down nordbahnstrasse walking the number 5 line
i walk alone no one on heinestrasse the rooms full of tarts
the air's dark i smoke cigarettes a few drags
i whistle and spit the butt out in front of me

i walk down nordbahnstrasse walking the number 5 line
the air's hot and even hotter in the pub i order a shot of rye
feed the machine and see the landlady's glazed eyes
i walk down nordbahnstrasse and it's night and i walk alone

WALTER BUCHEBNER

Above: a daughter of joy in the "Lambada Bar" on the Gürtel.
Opposite, above: clubbing in the Gasometer in Simmering.
Opposite, below: a tribune in the Krieau.

RETURN TO VIENNA

an early weary little flight or trip
flight by rail, transfer by city-jet
oh no, now I'm going to sneeze, back
in this Vienna of mine, my city, my over and out.

ERNST JANDL

Above: the auditorium of the Varieté Ronacher.
Opposite: the "Serapionstheater" in its new venue
at the Odeon (a former agricultural exchange).

The bibliographical references as listed correspond to the order of the texts in the book.

INGEBORG BACHMANN: City without surety! Selection of: The Thirtieth Year (transl. by Michael Bullock). N.Y. Holmes & Meier, 1987, 1995. Originally published in German as „Das dreißigste Jahr" © R. Piper & Co, Munich, 1961. English language translation copyright © 1964 by André Deutsch Ltd., London. Reprinted by permission of Holmes & Meier.

GASTONE BIGGI: Wien – nachklingend. In: Literatur und Kritik, Issue 151, June 1981, Otto Müller Verlag, Salzburg 1981

BERTHOLD VIERTEL: Wiener Pflaster. In: Das graue Tuch. Gedichte. Verlag für Gesellschaftskritik, Vienna 1994

GEORG KREISLER: Vienna, Vienna, Vienna. Selection from: Die alten bösen Lieder. (author's translation). Ueberreuter Verlag, Vienna 1989

ECKHARD HENSCHEID: Aus Wien schreibt mir ... In: Sudelblätter. © Haffmans Verlag AG, Zurich 1991

ERICH FRIED: Bekenntnis zu Wien. In: Gesammelte Werke, Gedichte I. Verlag Klaus Wagenbach, Berlin 1993

ERNST WALDINGER: Wienerisch. In: Literatur und Kritik, Issue 119, October 1977, Otto Müller Verlag, Salzburg 1977

EDMUND MACH: Hundertwasser. In: Buchstaben Florenz. Texte 1965–1979. Medusa Verlag, Vienna 1982

KARL KRAUS: Marmor-Chronik. In: „Die Fackel" No. 472/473, November 1917, p. 46 © Suhrkamp Verlag, Frankfurt/Main

WALTER BUCHEBNER: wien. In: Literatur und Kritik, June 1995, Otto Müller Verlag, Salzburg 1995 © Walter-Buchebner-Gesellschaft, Mürzzuschlag

BERTHOLD VIERTEL: Christkindlmarkt. In: Das graue Tuch. Gedichte. Verlag für Gesellschaftskritik, Vienna 1994

EDMUND MACH: Parlament. In: Buchstaben Florenz. Texte 1965–1979. Medusa Verlag, Vienna 1982.

KARL KRAUS: Der Verkehr. In: „Die Fackel" No. 315/316, 26. January 1911, p. 8 © Suhrkamp Verlag, Frankfurt/Main

ELFRIEDE GERSTL: Wien: Stadt mit Ärmelschoner. In: Wiener Mischung. edition neue texte, Linz 1982 © Elfriede Gerstl, Vienna

ALFRED POLGAR: Beethoven-Maske. In: Kleine Schriften 1. © Rowohlt Verlag, Reinbek 1982

ALFRED POLGAR: Denkmal. In: Kleine Schriften 1. © Rowohlt Verlag, Reinbek 1982

ERNST JANDL: du schönes wien ... In: Idyllen. Gedichte. Luchterhand Verlag, Darmstadt 1989

LUDWIG FELS: Höflichkeit. In: Blaue Allee, versprengte Tataren. © Piper Verlag GmbH, Munich 1988

GERHARD ROTH: Stephansdom. In: Reise durch das Innere von Wien. © S. Fischer Verlag GmbH, Frankfurt/Main, 1991

ILSE AICHINGER: Judengasse. From: Straßen und Plätze. In: Lebendige Stadt. Literarischer Almanach 1955, hg. vom Amt für Kultur und Volksbildung der Stadt Wien. Verlag Jugend & Volk, Wien 1955 © Ilse Aichinger, Wien

WOLFGANG GEORG FISCHER: Selection from: Mein Wienerlied der Gräber. In: Literatur und Kritik, issues 187/188, September/Oktober 1984. Otto Müller Verlag, Salzburg 1984

H. C. ARTMANN: dod en wossa. From: med ana schwoazzn dintn. © Otto Müller Verlag, Salzburg 1958

GASTONE BIGGI: Entlang der Donau. In: Literatur und Kritik, issue 155, 1981, © Otto Müller Verlag, Salzburg 1981

CHRISTINE BUSTA: Kleine Topographie des Wiederfindens. In: Literatur und Kritik, issues 195/196, June/July 1985, (cassette with nine volumes) © Otto Müller Verlag, Salzburg 1985, 1995

EDMUND MACH: Das verklungene Wien. In: Buchstaben Florenz. Texte 1965-1979. Medusa Verlag, Wien 1982 © Nervenheilanstalt Gugging, Haus der Künstler

ANDRÉ HELLER: Landschaft für Engel. In: Christine de Grancy: Hallodris und Heilige, Engel und Lemuren. Figuren auf den Dächern Wiens. Edition Wien, Wien 1994

HEIMITO VON DODERER: Historische Zeiten. In: Repertorium – ein Begreifbuch von höheren und niederen Lebens-Sachen. Dietrich Weber (Ed.). C. H. Beck'sche Verlagsbuchhandlung. München 1995

FRIEDERIKE MAYRÖCKER: wienumschlungen. In: Magische Blätter II. Suhrkamp Verlag, Frankfurt/Main 1987

INGE MERKEL: Selection from: Das Wiener Gift. In: Literatur und Kritik, issue 191/192, February/March 1985, p. 19 © Inge Merkel, Vienna

INGE MERKEL: Himmelserscheinungen. In: Das andere Gesicht. Residenz Verlag. Salzburg 1982

H. C. ARTMANN: schembrun. In: med ana schwoazzn dintn. © Otto Müller Verlag, Salzburg 1958

ROBERT SCHINDEL: Leopoldstädter Tanzlied. In: Geier sind pünktliche Tiere. Gedichte. Suhrkamp Verlag, Frankfurt/Main 1987

ALFRED POLGAR: Kastanie. In: Kleine Schriften 2. © Rowohlt Verlag, Reinbek 1982

ANTON KUH: Der wahre und der falsche Heurige. In: Zeitgeist im Literaturcafé. Löcker Verlag, Vienna 1983 © Verlag Kremayr & Scheriau, Wien

ROLF SCHNEIDER: Kaffeehaus. In: Leben in Wien. © Carl Hanser Verlag, Munich–Vienna 1994

WALTER BUCHEBNER: nordbahnstraßen-blues. In: Literatur und Kritik, June 1995, Otto Müller Verlag, Salzburg 1995 © Walter-Buchebner-Gesellschaft, Mürzzuschlag

ERNST JANDL: rückkehr nach wien. In: der gelbe hund. Gedichte. Luchterhand Verlag, Darmstadt 1980

The final curtain of the Staatsoper.

2nd edition 2000

Layout and jacket design by Andrea Schraml.
Editor of the German version: Brigitte Stammler.
Producer: Josef Embacher.
Photographic productions by Krammer Repro in Linz, Upper Austria.
Print: Studio Europa, Trient, Italy.
Translator of introduction, captions and the text on page 123: David P. Gogarty.
Translator of all other texts: Richard Sharp

Christian Brandstätter Verlagsgesellschaft m.b.H.
1080 Wien, Wickenburggasse 26
Telephone (+43-1) 408 38 14
Fax (+43-1) 408 72 00
e-mail: books@cbv.co.at